Natalie Ann Holborow is an award-winnii
Suddenly You Find Yourself was launched
Festival and listed as Wales Arts Review'
the *Cheval* anthology. Winner of the 2015 Terry Hetherington Award and a recent finalist in the Cursed Murphy Spoken Word competition, she blogs at www.natalieholborow.com where she shares her experiences and advice for aspiring writers.

Praise for *Small*:

'Rich and visceral in its imagery, Natalie Ann Holborow's *Small* wrestles the unruly body and mind through a world of food and wine from lemons to the dangerous fugu, peopled by self, lovers, family, and reinventions of literary and Biblical characters. She takes us on a journey of pain and recovery, as well as her travels. Her India poems are a sensual feast.' – **Kate Noakes**

'There is power in the everyday. Or rather, there can be. Hydrogen atoms always contained the potential to unmake the world, but it took the right kind of artist to unseam the nucleus and set the air on fire. Natalie Ann Holborow is that kind of artist. These poems are set in the world we know (a place where there are dishes to be done, parties to be had, inconvenient diagnoses, and a small voice inside your head, whispering doom) but they're guaranteed to blast you right out of it. There's a structural skill, here, that is hard to match. *Small* is atomic — in the best possible sense.' – **Bethany W. Pope**

'To be a woman means living in a body that is laid claim to by everyone under the sun. *Small* speaks to what happens when women are forced to live up to certain body ideals, which prize above all thinness and conventional femininity. Because so often, these poems tell us, we internalize the demand to keep ourselves small, to be shy, demure, not loud, not taking up space. *Small* reveals the narrator's struggle to overcome this, and also reminds us of the body's vulnerability in its poems about living with diabetes. Any woman will tell you that loving our bodies is a challenge, but *Small* reminds us that if women could, we could set this whole place on fire.' – **Zoë Brigley**

Small

Natalie Ann Holborow

PARTHIAN

Parthian, Cardigan SA43 1ED www.parthianbooks.com
First published in 2020
© Natalie Ann Holborow 2020
ISBN 978-1-912681-76-1
Editor: Susie Wildsmith
Cover design by Emily Courdelle
Typeset by Elaine Sharples
Printed and bound by 4edge Limited, UK
Published with the financial support of the Welsh Books Council British Library Cataloguing in Publication Data
A cataloguing record for this book is available from the British Library.

'Though she be but little, she is fierce.'
– **William Shakespeare,** *A Midsummer Night's Dream*
[Act 3, Scene 4]

For Mam: mother, friend, hero.

And for anyone struggling with their own Small.
I hear and I see you.

CONTENTS

NEVER DATE A POET

She says *never date a poet* / they are forever
bowling their souls through doorways /
cowering and wanting / staggering stairs
to the moon / perhaps then you will confide in her
you have always adored poets / the brute pen /

the velvet coat dropped from her back /
begging to be touched / the shelled knuckle
trawling the spine for hours / you will ask her
is that okay / dinner is a plate of impressionism / too sad to taste /
she will take a cold sip / carry your new face

on a plate / and write *okay* with her nail / between you
callas sigh out tedious eternities / water-jugs forever stagnating /
you say *so* / knowing the scrubbed red of her eye
marks two hysterical months of longing / she won't bother to engage /
the dull piano lulls and soothes / the slow salt snows

why do you not weep / her naked body a question mark
rising to meet you / bitter cold out and in / small cold gods
in bathrooms / cold hands / porcelain / some deeper chill
wafts back / holds you close / splayed on the bathroom mat /
hairs autograph the sink / nails scar the soap

perfume / shower-mist / the vulnerable wrist
dips to a drown / *why do you not weep* /
                    every pause is the end of the world.

GOOD MORNING, SMALL

We all have our favourite demons. Small is born
out of angles and nerves, has a brain

the weight of a fingernail. Clunks into life
like a terrible clock, counting the bars of her ribs.

Her Latin name cracks the throat, *Rex,* like a
dead lizard. She pins both arms like voodoo, nudges me

onto the scales. The light on her clavicle
hardens. She jabs. She giggles. She flounces.

The stupid act splits me to ounces.

HOW TO BREAK THE DIAGNOSIS

You announce the weight of the burden: an interminable
armful of books blotchy with diagrams, tugged desperately

from every shelf of the library, the inevitable search engine
interrogation. The patient sits upright like a child grown

clumsily into position, consigning herself to the language
of complex anatomy. Know there are ways to arrange

your face for delivering news on unseasonable summer
mornings, to make the tightening of the throat's cords slacken,

to create space to contain the patient in a room of slow dawning.

GIRL

Worship the towelled baby in her bubble of pram hoods
and milk, her mouth delicate as marigold. Worship innocence.
Worship her fist cracking crayons, her name no more
than a worm curled in the pattern of wallpaper
on her first day of school. Worship her pigtails.
Worship smallness. Worship the flat, clean island of her body,
worship her small shoes. Perch bows like birds in her hair.

Worship her crouched in the garden, tugging snails
and buttercups, lifting them slow to her eye.
Worship rag dolls. Worship monsters.
Worship the sundial of her shoe buckles,
size two, scuffed from scaling towers, dangling metres
of hair from the bedroom. Worship her knees.
Worship the tidy lawn of her tea parties,
worship her milk teeth. Worship wet cheeks.
Worship gingham. Worship the grimy crescents
of her nails. Worship the prints of her finger paints,
small as beans. Worship youth. Worship ignorance.
Send her safe to the homely corner
you keep empty for future ornaments.

SMALL CRASHES THE PARTY

This is just too sad for me   I say   listing every birthday
she has ruined   my ageing body split to photons
across the therapist's desk   each year's face thinning

fingers white against peeling vinyl   I have come to hate
this plastic chair   the heart's cleft splitting
as I turn back to watch myself   school-uniformed at my own party
grinning idiotic   lips raining cake   elastic
string of birthday hat splitting the pudge of my chin

there are no friends at the party   slyly I lick
powdered sugar off my thumb   clutching an ice-wet
tumbler of Diet Coke   Small sneaks in smelling of marzipan
the room is abundant with such punishments.

BATHING

I took to bathing at odd times of the night.
Pearls bumped my collarbones
like moonrocks, a big girl now
with the door slammed tight.
I dripped before the mirror,
became a woman.
At night, tired of wishing myself
slim as a cat's whisker, ribbon-thin,
I eased myself, girlish and shaking
into its waters, knuckled tea tree
into my hair. Unflexed my thighs.
Puffed out my belly at last.
Wiping the mirror
she found me like frost,
bath-wrinkled and laughing –
bent my bones to her
like brambles, like hunger.

FEAST

In a scuffed bungalow, a mile or so from the sea
I am shattering salt over parsnips, pricking sage
into blistered skin. A strand of herb curls in the heat.

Here there are ribbons of gravy, twisting like silk,
currants steaming from sponge. I move my fork
through potato, split its buttery heft,
the high waft of brandy burning from squat puddings,
slick bowls, spiralling from meticulous pastry.

Later, there will be chestnuts scooped
into papers, cradled like coals, toffees
sucked in a fug. Date-wrinkle. Sugar-dust.

Clementines thudding in bowls, untouched.

ANDROMACHE

Assume I am wearing black. Assume I have swathed myself
in the hollow shades of his bruised knees, dust-clogged and sticky,
assume I am leaching away with him. The tracks of his belly
      scar the dirt. Does anyone ask for his wife,

hair dripping over the Trojan walls, towering ten feet over
the beetled men below, gleaming up and blinking through her?
Assume the wind blew me over the edge of the wall, quiet
      and pale as salt. Hear me say nothing at all.

See these living hands. Hear the smack of my palms
against stone, blood coiling its way to my heart, bind me tough
as a horseman's rope. Blow my bones to polished pipes
      they play when great men fall. For me,

no tune at all if I should choose to stagger up,
sway on broken toes, burst my lungs screaming for
the dead man's bones with our only child tumbling
      over crumbling stone in a gasp of blood and milk.

When Hector cracked his back behind the chariot,
when the bruises flowered blue, when our only baby spiralled
like sycamore, the Gods, I felt it too – I called *Astayanax,*
      I called *Hector.* Who called *Andromache*? Who?

ROMEO

These days, Juliet forgets on purpose
        to draw the curtains, smacks
her thighs, talcumed and pink,
armpits still crackling
        with bubbles. Every night,

she hoists one leg
        over the footstool she's dragged
whispering across the carpet
to the balcony window, angled
        just so. Lifts a whip of lotion

and rubs. Each calf tightens,
        gleams, and Romeo
poor Romeo
circles the bushes below
        waiting for a glimpse

of bare arse, nubbed breasts,
        nipples stiffening
on powdered ribs. A smudge of oil
glistening on one clean shoulder.
        Tell them Romeo,

in fourteen lines only
        kill it with a couplet
tell them all
        about love at first sight.

DIAGNOSIS

10th December 1998

The doctor shows us a cartoon kid
half-naked, grinning stupidly from ear-to-ear
with all her guts on show. He points out
the pancreas, a slimy cluster of grapes
about this size, squeezes his fist to demonstrate
so I do the same with a tiny hand, wince
as the cannula shifts. He tells me

it's okay to feel confused, that
it's *a lot to take in* but he's talking
now to my parents, trying to smile,
eyes hardened to moons. I ask
to go home, but there are things to do,
blood rolled to a miniscule ruby, balled
at the end of my finger. Voodoo pins
to master. *Do you understand?*

We sit in silence on the drive home,
hands raw and wringing. Mam's handbag
trills with needles, slim vials of insulin
a parting gift. I panic about blood glucose,
my sorry bones, arse bruised like a plum
from the car seat. For a moment I am glad
I don't get it. Mam smokes the shock for us
through the window of Dad's Mondeo.
We discuss anything but this bunch-of-grapes
useless inside me, a bobbing goldfish flipped over.

COUNTING MYSELF TO SLEEP

Like babies, they cried for attention, begged to be counted—
white, wholesome cries that had us
crossing the bed's divide. *Jump!* I bellowed
as tonight's arrived, wrinkling their velveteen noses.
They stood at the gate, dumb-tongued, refusing
to lift their legs, so I straddled the fence,
limbs loose and dripping in a field of stupid sheep.
I do this over and over: count myself to sleep.

THE OTHER SIDE OF THE MOON

We rear the ladder against the moon,
perch owls through incessant coaxing,
the silver drum-majors, the ceremonial scene –
some say it's like filling and emptying a dam,
this ebbing light, this summit of perfection
where we go trawling the spinal glow,
the invisible neck, over the precise seacoal dark
where the imagined face of goddess or baby
endures smoking horizons, calmly refrains
from dying at dawn. Later, the sky will boil gold,
the tawnies will squat back to sleep.
The sacred note, clear as brass, will flush out
the night, loosen the ladder's squeeze. Cold
is the music of car horns and larks, a groan
of rising heads. The other side of the moon
hiccups with dust, decides to remain a mystery.

GESTALT THERAPY

tell me / what does the chair mean / the cloud
coloured padding / *headshake* / wind slapping
sad bluebells / okay then / what does the word
apricity taste like / *warm skin and apricots* /

but back to the chair / can you calcify it
to a wishbone / tell me can you put
a person on it / *she doesn't ask what the chair*
tastes like / old nuts and dust / iron tang /

has she ever even met a metaphor /
what is empathy / *earth roots / wires*
hissing dirt / the mad garden hand
patting / wet compost fists / what colour

is empathy / *wipe old nuts and dust*
from my tongue / citalopram weighs
an eyeful of coins / tell me / *no tell me /*
ever snapped a chair leg and felt it

SMALL AND THE BIRDS

she says *who is Small* / Small is not me
but part of me / sweeps from me
like a headrush / calcified grin / all twirls
and jabbing angles / slithery wings / *like a crow* /
no not like a crow / she points at the bird outside
it blurs in the rain / feathers and trash / hot static /
or a snake / no not a snake / its unassuming coil
has no capacity for scrabbling the way she does /
sticky-nailed / chain-mail of frost pricking the neck
besides why does the owl not swoop her away / *do you*
ever feel like an owl / I tick the box *no never an owl* / Small
hoots softly at my back / froths a ring of feathers
at her throat / says we shouldn't talk about her like this

BODKIN

Twice a day I take a trip to the annexe toilets
for insulin, hold the hypodermic needle
like a bodkin. Afterwards, I watch
the bug of blood track my belly
in a relieved little puff,
crush it just short of the waistband.

BLACKMAIL

There is wattage in the paper that pools on our doormats.
Each cursive adds its miniature current to things
spelled out in code, or at worst, unspoken,

the speculative mail bag that swings in the forest
unable to bear its own gravity, each stopped utterance
dropping to earth in the form of snow.

Who could believe such pauses were nothing more
than electric stunning the mouth, a bulb of lime,
a sharpness that rucks itself to silence?

This is something. Our ears follow the trail knowingly,
the brain translating each deadweight hesitation
to matter, licked postage, something new to say.

RUNNING

must be doing something because
now I'm crying
over the smell of fresh laundry,
the sweet folds, warm, *soft*
as a baby's arse
and the woman
in the garden, tugging towels
from the wind,

    running
past pubs
where someone's father
fossilised on a barstool,
picks beermats
to mosaics. He presses
the wet rags
to his fingertips,
a pad of roughened skin,
but doesn't notice me

    running
through whirlwinds of litter,
tugging my ponytail tight
the dark thatch
of telephone wires
humming with gossip,

    running,
ziplining
the fragile stalk of someone's
tenth cigarette
in a car park, as they
shield the struggling
light. It shrivels out

into ashes, whispers
back into the wind
where I'm

        running
to forget
the hollow places,
the neat ounce of your life.

SOMETIMES, YOU CRY IN THIS CAR

The great shivery out-breath that tries to bear
the world's ache comes rasping out again
then backs up into silence, waiting to fall into memory-trap.
It makes no sense: heat murmuring on the bonnet of the car,
its deaf engine that might have once roared
into summer, the sunlight on its registration plate like houseflies
on butter. Sometimes, you cry in this car
with the engine off and that feeling you sometimes get
like stepping into a cramped elevator, a train
without any schedule, both hands on the wheel sticky
as though you'd pressed them too long
against the shimmering fever of the universe.

TEN MINUTES

Joseph Plunkett and Grace Gifford married at Kilmainham Gaol in 1916 on the day of Plunkett's execution. They were granted only ten minutes together before Plunkett's death.

Grace counts a knuckle
for every minute,
the dull thud of his pulse
    in her hand.
Wedding bands
stiffen their fingers.
Time scatters—
    one minute,
        two minutes,
           three—

the guard puffing clouds in his collar.
Stars cram above the Liffey
where children crouch
    or scuttle back home
to the dark. Ash rain.
Smoke-signals
    —four minutes,
        five minutes,
           six—
the rivers bend and kiss.

In Kilmainham we bent
shivering in the doorway,
    palms pressed in the other's hand
and saw in the stone
Joe on the floor with a blanket
heaped upon him like earth,
    a candle stammering grace.

For ten minutes,
we walked between gallows,
        sad crosses
rising stark
as two Pole Stars
—seven minutes,
        eight minutes,
                nine.

A soldier stands by
        with a fixed bayonet,
prowling the edge of his watch.

SMALL TAKES A BATH

Small falls into bubbles   tumbling
        in a slow arc   skin flaking like slate
      approaching the molten core of the earth   the depths
of the world have a certain smell   like copper   or black holes

or pearls of dead glamour   do you remember how
        I dug my nails in your hand   your fingers
    plunging like divers   steaming clear   *get out*
of the bath you'd said   pulling my hair   tugging it like a plug

huge useless saviour   invisible ship trailing rainbows
        in haloes   there are chains down here   soapy gods
    angels blooming enormously   Small wrings her hair
smoothes her crown   a wet skull makes a mortal of anyone

LEMONS

After my blood has swirled away
into ribbons in the phlebotomist's hand,

weeks after the sorry rub
of the nurse's palm on my bicep,

I cradle a steel bowl. Whisk. Weigh
lemons in each hand.

As I lean in silence, swing open the latch
to a birdless yard,

stiff and creased with winter,
the lemons sweat in their pans.

The batter rises, bubbled and sweet.
A small and absolute thing.

MESSAGE

When I drop my bags at the door
up go his bull-horns, wrestling me
to reason. Outside, a crow flashes
through a streetlight, existing briefly.
Palpitation. Wine-slap. Something
unspoken tosses between us, buoyed
upon the familiar house-smell of lemons,
shoes, the humid post-vacuum musk.
He hasn't kissed me in a fortnight.

Come Saturday night a downpour
roars godly through the ceiling, so I let it
spray a white plume at my shoulder
while he roosts, tapping his phone beneath
bedsheets. A firework spatters the windows.
Another girl, peering out, can keep a secret;
his phone a stone skipping a message
across to her; orchestral static between us,
sheering bone-bright through the dark.

THERE ARE NO DAFFODILS IN VARANASI

We tumble out, sticky as *gulab jamun*
in the fug of Indian heat, shrug beneath our luggage
as though we can squirm the temperature down.
Banaras. Cobras lift from jars in the *Assi Ghat,*
roped in a small girl's fingers where she squats
over scattered rice. I gasp, point out the monkey
picking dreadlocks on the charmer's shoulder,
crease a rupee into his palm. He meets my eye,
namaste, and the monkey screams.

Remember, on the Ganges, how we shivered
into photographs for Mam, for Dad, to show them
that same sun that will melt their frozen driveways,
warm their valleys. There are no daffodils in Varanasi.
Marigolds cluster like barnacles against rowboats,
where the bare-bellied boys don't notice, stopping
to tug the fishes, easy as loose teeth. India talks in her sleep.

RED FORT

It is raining in Old Delhi. Our Welsh baritones bubble
like lentils on ladles, swoop across streets, a brief *shwmae*
for their sundial stare, toddlers tucked behind skirts. A shrivel
of marigold peels in the dust. They trail like tails from baskets,
splashed, punctuating brown clouds sputtered from tuk-tuks,
unspooling from joss-sticks, hostels half-shuttered
against the low-hanging sun, India's bright eye. Ghee-sizzle.
Tyre-screech. The heaving cattle steam and piss, birds cruising
their bovine hips. This morning, we splashed to our knees
to scale minarets, windowless towers,
soaked our skins like honeyed bread. Smoke and stairwells.
We were blind inside pillars, paprika-red. A voice
from the Tawe wrings itself out, tries slowly in Hindi instead.

AFTER INDIA

They are stopped bells, forever tilted mid-swing,
fat scarves gagged around their mouths
like coughing guppies. They swim politely. They scull
through smoke, all bobbled cotton
and business suits, puffed *mornings* they don't mean,
rattling their umbrellas in doorways.
You settle back, dab pastry on your finger.
　　　Think from your owl-brown hat

of the Sundarbans, of long white crocodiles
dragging their bellies and smiling, think of hornets
long as darts. Shape Calcutta with your one gloved
hand against the window, rub the snouts of dirty dogs
with sugared thumbs. You are stinking of culture and *jhal muri*,
the *Tawe* for the iron slug of the Ganges. For the boys
tugging fish like teeth or beggar's rupees. Bowl-bellied,
　　　face streaked, a shaggy tiger of a man

waves you back to Varanasi from your air-conditioned carriage,
temples shoving to the heavens between the BT building
and the sea. Spit sandalwood onto your wrists
after India. Crease marigolds and ash into your fists.

PANIC BIRD

I'd gone on and on about the dog
in meticulous detail / drunk coffee
I shouldn't be drinking / spoon-quake /
blood-hammer / Colombian tang /

described this creature loping
towards me every night / slab-tongued /
galleon-black / a hulking lump of astronomy /
his massive paws eclipse the world / moonless

but the black dog doesn't play fetch / bounds away
when I call / instead / please say hello
to my panic-bird / *who's-a-pretty-boy-then* / swelling
mango-bright on my shoulder / crows words

like *emergency* / *smoke* / my hot little rooster
pecking my femurs to flutes / *who's a pretty—*
nip it in the beak like this / pinch keratin
between my fingers / all night it sings

like a maniac / half-dreams of nosebleeds /
leaks / giggling executions / hits the high notes
with leaping lungs / wattle / blood-feathers
glued to my skull / I am crowing back

inside four walls / sterile grey / *who's-a-pretty—*
dear God look what it's done / pinned my shape
against pinewood / flapping / pecking / my skull spills
forth its mute yolk / begging for dogs in the dark

SMALL VISITS THE BAKERY

Small does things that shrink me to a flour mite.
I haven't got the energy to carry her home
in a shopping bag, sharpened bones, a brain
microscopic. *Doesn't she know there are people*
starving on the streets, says a voice from the queue.
Hot belly rising, a woman laughs, chewing a cloud
of baguette. When she smiles, a sunflower seed
pokes from her teeth like a stiffened moth,
pinned between her incisors. Doesn't she know,
I am freezer-mist. I am thin as a pocket of cellophane.
The oven smoke chokes me with comforts.
Small springboards from bread roll to bread roll,
kicking flour as she goes.

FUGU

It takes years of skill to gut *fugu*
but he can do things with knives, work

quickly, faithful blade tempered
to a keen edge. Deep slicks of oil, fish

big as a paper moon, we curl steam
along bowls of *dashi*, catch the other's eye
      like sudden hooks
            and bite.

SMALL SWALLOWS A FLY

Tonight we are having wine for dinner   our favourite
plum-shine   wet lacquer   we could even pretend
we are swimming   foxy reds   oak-smoke
cool odours of vanilla rising   *let's wander vineyards*
in dark skirts   I tilt the glass to my lips
gulp downwards   flush upwards   pour another

Small licks a peanut   puffs her cheeks   sometimes
Small tells jokes with her breath   or apes about
pretending to be humongous   one time we drowned a fly
with wine-drops   trying to get it drunk   *the drops* she said
are lava   running her fingers along the menu   she dared me
to eat the fly   *you*   no, you   sweat broke out on me   blood

slugged along the arteries   I drank until the blood was wine
moths as big as hands swarmed the lamps   and later
counting *three, two, one*   giggling like clocks   Small and I
pressed a wing   to each of our tongues   swallowed the fragile lace

THE VISIT

Gabriel lifts his hand to the door, deciding
between knuckling the wood politely
or splitting the walls like an orange,
his glorious wings, their whalebone solidity
splayed like snapdragons, or perhaps
sinking through the ceiling to surprise her
in a cloud of auric smoke, trumpet
pressed to his mouth. Mortals, he knows,
are skittish, sweep rings around bedrooms
with sage sticks to kill the dead. The scant wisp
of a shadow and they're stiff in their tracks
inside mirrors, hysterical as bees, so he fills
his lungs for the hell of it, puffs out
a desert breeze, swears to God
he will fix the roof on his way out.

GABRIEL

Gabriel is slumped now, rolling stars between his fingers,
waiting for a cry. All night long he has stalked the hills,
startled sheep, washed his wings in bitter streams.
Squeezed clouds with shaking hands. The labour was long.
Joseph had set down his wood-blocks, stood uselessly
between woman and manger, patted Mary's fists. In a stable
bent like a tired horse, a saviour flings out his limbs,
gasps for air, kicks miracles into straw. Kings scarper
like geckos through deserts. Shepherds quake in the dark.
Gabriel yanks out his trumpet, puffs its dusty note.
At this sudden art, the world turns its head
from the stuporous earth, lilies twisting for rain.

THE MAGI

A star holds its stubborn distance.
Given long enough, even wisdom
whittles to small talk, a passing grunt,
the hot wheeze of camel-breath
putrid at noon. Gold rubs at his thighs.
Frankincense spritzes a wrist.

The moon melts nightly
across deserts, slow fires
wagging bright in the dunes —
at the child's sudden cry, pure as milk,
a pale eye crisps with wonder,
weeps light across colder heavens.

ALMOST

When the sickness is gone, only heat is left.
In the panting rooms, when my vest peels
like chicken skin, I might walk about the house naked
or in a sheet, imagine my belly swelling out
like a winning watermelon. Stop every now and then
to test my breasts for sheer agony. *Look,* I say
while he dozes, *I am growing a miracle.* His pretence
wanes thin within weeks. Lighter than dust, soon
you are nothing but a flare of dull crosses, wet blues
soaked onto sticks, the wisp of a sigh unbreathed.

SMALL SENDS HIM PACKING

Impossible, he said, *for any man*
to pick a fight with her and think
he's won. Small claws out
from an overnight bag,

slithers between us like a daft child
how can I reach you (he aims for
the small hoop of my waist and misses)
when she's circled you in glass and marrow?

He is demanding and she a storm
giggling in his face on borrowed breath,
pounding her feet rhythmically, softly,
into the sift of the pillow, feathers tossed

coughing between us. White noise.
Blind with panic, he reaches over,
clamps my wrist too urgently
and startles her into fury

so we lie there with no option
but to watch her dig for my skeleton,
Mercury crashing slowly in retrograde,
tiny volcanoes crowning in the dark.

GRIEF

Maybe God will do something
with the flaccid roses, freeze

their necks, spit miracles
into the jug and bring them back,

little macabre thorns, fire-skirts.
Something naked and spectral

rises from the earth, materialising
like ectoplasm from a waiting room

seance. A wilting acquaintance
says something kind because you're gone.

I am not certain of any of these things.

I am biting hard on a candle, joking
about smoking it like a finger-thick

cigarette, I am slamming a window shut
to keep out sunsets. I am peeling a lily

open, splaying its early tinge.
I am changing the subject to nothing.

Nobody knows what to do with me.

BROKEN EGGS

Pressing my nose to the world
she says *this is now,* my breath
steaming futures onto windows,

says *waiting is dying*
then giggles herself
hysterical over cobbles,

ankle-soaked. She bellows
to rouse the living, more ghost
than she is, plunged

ten minutes into the future
with knotted guts. Panic birds.
Wet feathers and endings.

The lesson is this:
time curls minutes
around wrist-bones,

so I snatch at my arm,
pull gold with my hand,
but for all my grasping,

it's like trying to pull
whites from broken eggs.

SMALL BREAKS A VOW

And we want you to say she's so tiny her body slithers away
like a ribbon, the familiar dissolution of water

hissing in shallows. Grief makes us wander.
Small rubs my fingers, hugs my waist, asks for my hand

in marriage, then bursts out laughing. Flops seaweed-hair
over my face. We go with him later, invisibly, to where he is not

crouching in the crocuses, one knee covered in sawdust.
He is in the car, already driving away from this horrible thing

cleaved to my waist, tangling herself in my hair. He floors the car,
a scarlet blur. Small waves. *It probably didn't happen*, Mum says,

heartbreak makes you see things that aren't there but Small is there
all lopsided, gnawing on my fingers, peeping out like a crooked tooth.

To prove it she suddenly sneezes. A million vows
                                go blasting out of my mouth.

DIALLING TONE

We are warbirds flying down
phones from separate homes.
Me, sudden and huge in my childhood bed,
you storming what used to be ours. Mark
your territory in the boots you'd scrub
twenty times in one night, calling me
obsessive over a hiss of brushes.

Tea soaks into the carpet. Steam
goes spiralling out of you.
But here, in the debris – toppled
bookshelves, sloshed wine – we tug wires
across cities, disconnect ourselves
with umbilical precision.

She tells me, robotic, the next day
and the day after that, and even half a year later
to leave a message, an on-the-spot
improvised monologue you will shoulder
to your ear while you dress, something
to forget again as soon as your boot is tied.

ATTICS

Patience is holy to any woman
who summons the past from attics.

Each plastic bulb blinks its cheap eulogy.
Every wreath rounds out, crying your vowel.

I started digging for you amongst the tinsel,
each memory's wizened foil –

the neat white envelope peeking out
from a squat of poinsettia,

fished from a thatch of plastic pines,

a papered box, the star of Bethlehem
glittering wryly inside.

The moon's bright curtain snows coldly
around my shoulders, tells me

time heals slower than it can build
its quiet stratum of dust.

RELAPSE

As the ferns glitter and stiffen, you'll pray for me
cleaved to the radiator, turning a book with my feet,

my fingers shoved like razor clams
behind coat-sleeves.

You'll pray for my bones dragging themselves to the bathroom,
my hand tugging the light, searching the pristine step

for my value in pounds. The dial
flickers. I lift my toes.

Every morning, I harvest myself: carry the web
of my tendons, gently pluck out the heart.

It flops miserably in my palm. Time now to weigh
the ounce of my life, blow

into dust and bone.

FROST

Morning steams out, nimbus-faced,
shower-misted, ringing snowdrops in her fists.

Slow herons. The river's glass unravels
its chain of minnows, salt-silvered,
lapping the low wall, tightly-bricked,
chilled to a knife-edge

and the crows with their eyes of onyx
go swerving like planets, a cacophony
of shadow rustling through sleet. Cobbles
shine with haloed heat, reddening pickets

like tinder. Gently melting frost
from the salted roads of winter.

I run twenty miles that afternoon
in the slanting rain   backslashes   who knew
tiny towns could have such dark perimeters
in early spring the cows are slow   silky-uddered
I lap them steaming across meadows
wet pastures hot milk smell chugging in clouds
I slap at my fringe   scatter beads of clear drizzle
the bulls are thick and fierce   stocky trunks
shunting the cold hills   I sprint harder   hair flapping
like a sparrow trapped   and sometimes   on days
like these I am a bird   hatching in reverse   crunching
the shell back whole   I've outrun the dumb cattle
but really all this   the dull beat of my heel   scuff
of gravel   is rain gone about erasing   each toppled stone
dulling to a warning   habitual isolation   eighteen miles
is an act of casual hell   immutable famine   at twenty
I say   it will happen   the drizzle suffused
to a smirr   a dark candelabra of yews   I reel
to a halt at twenty   a bull stops dead on a hill

SMALL LOSES SLEEP

Small doesn't let me sleep
    in the small hours
playing the accordion
    of my waist
thumping a xylophone
    out of my vertebrae

its celestial echo
    startles the wind
sometimes I dream
    of tapeworms writhing
and pale as string
    or of exoskeletons

some cumbersome scarab
    glutted on flesh
getting fatter
    only on the inside

ENTERING THE BED IS LIKE
ENTERING A CAR PARK IN FROST

When I return at last and move about the room
making shallow conversation, you pretend not to see
as I shed my dress, slacken my posture, all at once
unwelcome and cold, like snow folding on the driveway.
Entering the bed is like entering a car park in frost.
Later, I'll make sculptures of you, compress your nose
to new angles, realign the ribs, rub those sleepy eyes
until that stare is no longer your own
and your confusion begins to startle me.

ADDERS

He's shoved up against my face now, unavoidable, familiar, like staring
at a puncture on the cap of my own knee, bent double, stuffed
in a battered trunk. This is my half of our life, killed and bagged,
swallowed whole like a mountain goat. After love it's so hard
to digest the evidence. I was always so good at pointing out adders,
their lovely diamond heads, copper scales. A silent river of chains.
I lift boxes, searching the way I'd learned, for basking geometry,
the sly giveaway coil, imagining for a moment the one broad sweep
that had gathered it all, a snap of the jaw, a *right that's it* sandstorm
raging through the house, culminating in a brief temper of chair legs,
hairbrushes, scarves frothing against the flanks of a desert sidewinder
until I'm forced to gut boxes in my childhood room, a knife-wielding
lunatic, slicing the bellies of boas. For hours, I pluck the shreds of myself
I thought he'd swallowed forever – a tile of skin splayed across a love note,
a false nail glugged in a paperweight, a kidney slick in a wineglass – coolly
lifting them free, but always one eye swung open for adders – curling awake
from houseplants, cups, the skull of a goat, the husk of a lover's skin.

HYPERGLYCAEMIA

on the perpetual night shift I've done everything I can
to stay awake   stooped with a brush   shaken
bloodied strips into bin-bags   the crooked hooks
of dud needles squashed roses of blood on my fingertips
I blast the tap violently   knuckle-smudge my eyes
piss twenty times in one night   still sucking my finger
go back to the tap   catch water in my mouth and swell
like Ouroboros feeding on itself in the hidden places
of the world   my body chewed to angles   spokes and bone
filling and flushing forever   *I will never not be thirsty*
I say   sucking my spit   still gritty with sugar and blood

CWTCH

For Roisin and Zoe

The radius of sisters has expanded to hold you,
convenes and relinquishes form, a circumference
of tides turning to each other always in a summer
grown out of gold and dull confinement. In the pauses
that follow phonecalls, there are gaps that pour
salvaged dialogue into wine glasses, the edges
of which would sing if only we could strike them
once more in gardens, as if this were still
the time of year for daisies rankling the legs
of wooden tables, the silky exhalation of menthols
struck in the glowing smoking shelter
of the Lexington, four glasses down, dusk drawing
its drapes like a crinoline skirt. A snake-pit of chains
flashing gaudily in the neon glare of lights. Or perhaps
this time we're ankle-deep in the fattened swell of Gower,
paperchain gulls pinioned across horizons, stretched
between salt-gales, unspooling from nicotine, a lesson
in sing-song accents. *Cwtch:* a word you've long mastered.

SMALL LEARNS THE CHAKRAS

She occupies a seven-storey space
at the top of a high-rise tower block,
some sly geological outcrop and I'm made
to breathe into all seven storeys. Inside,
on the fifth floor, Small is yelling

what the fuck are these coloured lights—
you are colourless! Look. A bulb swings
from the fleshy swell of my epiglottis
but does not light. Small smacks
through my tongue like a trapdoor.

Tell her then. I look up through my fringe.
A bored therapist isn't looking, painting
the world on her shoe with a lazy blink. *Listen,*
I say. She starts, reddens like traffic,
loose hairs curling in the heat. *The colours*
are all turned off in me, why must we pretend—

Small nods her head, bounces tauntingly
between my teeth. The therapist turns off the tape,
starts talking blue throats, spinning lights
but I don't tell her how sometimes I hear
stems gasping for air in supermarket buckets
or taste arsenic in water. *How does blue feel?*

She wants the words *calm, easy.* Small squeezes
my neck, fields ropes between her claws.
                    The fifth chakra is the colour of choking.

PHYSICAL

And despite everything, I seek comfort
in the physical; hairy clouds of shaving foam

fuzzing forever down the plughole, the last
of your aftershave dissolved into atoms,

collar-starch, a loose pubic hair whittled
to wire. I pinch it between my nails,

hold its kink to the light. A scrap of you
I can hold tight. This, even this, is something.

MIMICKING ROMANCE

We've debated ice cream flavours, *would-you-rather,*
crunched out our cigarettes in a parasol stand. You said
you'd rather be a snail than a worm, *it would be like
showing off a new car,* then asked which one I'd rather be.

I think, jangling ice-blocks with a paper straw, I'd rather be
lifting a slug like a flaccid tongue, or inhaling deep the fug
of a freshly-peeled boot, than here on a grotty patio,

mimicking romance with you.

BETTER LIES

Sticking with the lie, I liked it.
A sly waiter brings us brandy and ice
a sliver of wet lemon

I say the best
painting I ever did was dusk rolled red
along the *Assi Ghat*
       the steady fire
that frilled its heat along the mangroves.
I lift the lemon to my lips and make it smile.
You grope for an ashtray, click your lighter

shield its wagging heat against the wind
and ask if you can see it.
       See what?

The painting.
       I shake my head
look out at a street freckled with gum
lined with pawn shops and flimsy houses.

In another place there was saffron and silk
       bleating goats
moon-white *lassis* and fragrant cones
of *jhal muri*

a hand plucking an orange
free from a pyramid
but I never painted those
       no never

I've never painted a thing in my life
but I say it anyway
I say I painted a masterpiece

because always there is someone
            offering sharper lemons

better lies.

SMALL VISITS THE CLINIC

For a sick girl, I have unsinkable hands.
    They announce themselves in rings
around the red place where it hurts,
each hand spinning itself through empty air,
    redrawing pain into borders, each loop
swooping ever more theatrically than the last
with an effort I seem to wince into

carving maps from the hidden dune of the hip,
    sweeping flanks into rivers, the rib's
whitened tine that slices so alarmingly
through the fine blue cotton of my favourite shirt
    and its slackened buttons. Never here
of her own accord, a frowning Small
clings to the sealed door, spreads her claws flat

listening in through the wood, never hearing a thing
but air whizzing clean through my fingers
    to show them right where it hurts.

DEFEAT

Days, weeks, months, then the astonishment of sudden loss,
leaving me piecing together what I'd seen with the window
unrolled, smoking numbly in the hospital car park post-visit.
The sun is rising behind me, the longest night commencing
its slow evaporation into light, the dawn's fresh oblivion.

Not for the first time, the moon has a face that says
you get used to it. I mumble something to a shower
of starlings tumbling to earth, pressing their heads
to the ground, looking for signs of life: sparse shrubbery,
the crimp of a worm on dry concrete, perhaps asking them

how can such a thing be numbed, as if begging nature
to explain the ferment of passion, the almond-wrinkled
heart, wrists slackened from the pinion of self-restraint.
After the first heartbreak, the body stands up with a mouthful
of dark, puts one foot in front of the other, and is gone.

VICTORIA TERRACE

Tap splutters and spits
in a shared bathroom, too grey,
bleachy Atlantic. She twists
the handle: fizzing jets.
Takes too long. Listen:
group uproar, letters splashed
over side tables,
closed doors. Towel rub.
Mould blooms green as a banknote.

                              You are big now,
                         sophisticated. Look at you,
                          cracking dry spaghetti:
                              thin, wheaty bones
                         over pans, sputtering gas
                    and grease-ring Michelin stars.
                         Popping lids from jars,
                    buggy mushrooms. Bean-slop.
                    Eating well, Mam. Eating well.

Is this the dream then,
this flaking, shuddering house,
moth-freckled, damp-bottomed
and senile? Something still beats
in the scarred white walls,
boot-bruises. Fractured doors,
unhinged. Breakfast eaten shyly
in the wrong language, stiff
in marijuana haze. Wrench
open the skylight. Intruding rain.

Around her wet mangle
of clothes, a housemate hums.
A native tune perhaps, her
Polish eyes lost in her head.
Her thin limbs in the early hours
stretch and lift, and there you are
with your ratty eye
meeting her ice-blues. Cold
as this salty sea-town,
your frozen home.

SMALL PULLS MY HAIR OUT

I'm infatuated with these few thin strands
kimonoed in tissue and laid flat, loosened

from my head in one sweep. Sudden fractures.
Useless floss. The naked shrink of trodden roots

loosening hold of their follicles. Holding the brush
after one last sweep, I thrash it against the light.

Brown threads drift from the bristles.
       A brief chill flushes my skull.

HAIRCUT

I cut my hair with sure, chunky snips over the sink
like snipping the ends from spring onions. I'd been warned
it would come to this, water sprinkling
from the blades, the hair, exhausted, dropping ribbons
onto white acrylic. My wits blown away like owls.

Look, each heavy lock shines in a golden light,
sublimely, leaking from above, so I feel cheered
against my will. The last hanging thread of integrity.

What other news from the neighbourhood
of grim revelations? The bells are stunned
in their churches. The postman tramps along
the railway line, hoping for a journey, elbows
rustling against a green breeze. I open the window
and wave. *Look,* I am saying, *this is giving up.*

BREATHLESS

She has curled back into herself, an old baby reversing.
Buoyed on the ward, sob-soaked, breathless, a pillow
palms her heavy head, her body a slumped bag. Our third night

rolls long and fretting on hospital benches, pricking stars
out of car parks, scouring clipboards for miracles, knowing
but not saying, *there is nothing to save the drowned*, the lungs'
slow sea forever filling, rain-pearled carnations bleach and wheeze,
a green breeze floating over her in ribbons. *Is this enough?* you ask,
flicking absently to a tired sun, illuminating clear opiates, watching
the thick drip of doses buying time, a minute for a milligram.

Her eyelids flush shut like a plastic doll. This is a final thing.
To feel the room unglue around me, loving her terribly,
left living, feet slipping on the morning's circled soap
        hurts worse than the frozen in-breath.

HEMKOMST

In memory of Anthony Jones

The tarred knotholes of pine and spruce
still carry the whorl of your fingerprints
in that photograph we took, poets belted
by the arms on summer lawns. Crisp
Swedish phrases raced home in your case,
pungent with woody glamour. *Min vän. Hem.*

But this was never your homecoming was it,
these tired cobbles, tin-sheet rain, crabs bumping
their claws against stone. No, your *hiraeth*
rolled wide the steam of glassy lakes, steadier
than these drab elements of cockles and salt, superb
little thin-legged warblers. They wade into estuaries
browner than earth, gasp mouthfuls of mud and silt.

What had been tumbling in those small-hour filaments,
what had your pen been churning? *Nothing,* you laugh,
in Tranås again, still with your cigarette burning.

FOUNTAINS

So here you are again, brilliant as a fountain
spilling into its own circumference, yet the heart
like a pool boiling dry, having given too much
for too long. The ripples suffuse until the ache of it
hauls you to ground, those times when you feel nothing
but the weight of waterfalls above you, the corralled
selves you've invented for yourself out of sheer panic.

On these nights where you run from the dark, even
the frosted halo of moon will feel like a stranger
beckoning, the affirmation you need that life goes on.
Know this: that light still refracts from certain
facets of the planet, that water can carry invented
selves back to the heart of a fountain,
that the spring-green eyes are perfectly equipped
to see truth in reflection, should they choose to.

THE ROBIN

The size and shade of a chocolate heart,
its blood-bib flushes frost, scrapes ice
like card glitter from winter boughs.

They say the robin is a telegram,
lifted by feather and bone
across the sacred light of divides.

And then there's you.

Dressing-gowned on the porch,
blinking gold into time, you listen out
for birdsong, for fountains oozing to life.

In the presence of vermilion
there's always one message
that spins from the wind

on a feather, one particular face
rearranging itself, bird-stippled
and freezing, finding shape

in the origami snow.

SMALL GETS ADMITTED

Small kicks me, crawling
to Accident & Emergency
at one in the morning.
My stomach, I explain,
*is a scoop of coals
steaming.* The doctor
is baffled, places a hand
where thin fingers lie,
tearing me inside out
like a net of tigers
escaping. A tinder-chewing

Small drags her marks
like hieroglyphs
unseen in the hollows,
squat as a rock, tonguing
the length of my backbone.
She bucks out a heel
for attention, puffs
at tiny coals. *Witches,* I say
to the doctor, dousing
myself with antacid,
burned exactly like this.

CONFESSION

I never wanted a wedding
an interminable dazzle
          of absurd headwear
a monstrous procession of skirts
          I never wanted

to strut and twist
limbs posed, a doll in the mirror
blowing my nails
toes curling

each hair corkscrewed, tugged
          and sizzled to a thunderbolt

nor did I want to be released
coolly from my father's arm
to a polished altar

catching my heel in a hook of lace
foaming forward
          face erased
the organ's dusty pipes wheezing dust
          Pachelbel's *Canon in D*
          the disappointed note huffing from a cross

          nor did I want
to trail clouds
of gypsum, lily of the valley
arrogant fistfuls scratching my palms

and believe me Father
          I never wanted him lifting the veil
kissing me slowly
licking his name

　　　　damp and deliberate along my lips
I try it now

suck in air
spit it back out
my name scrubbed off
　　　　for two tedious syllables
when Judas leaves I weep
　　　　　　　at the miracle.

SMALL GETS RESUSCITATED

Curtain snatched upward in a gust of emergency / ribs split
    like a binder / someone tugs up her sleeve / there it is

more bruise than roses / her tattoo sputters back into bloom / slick
    dab / pricked vein / dry snaps of breath / the multitudinous dead

trudge to her bedside / slab-toed / hunched waiting and snug
    in death-bags / feet reeking of latex and moss / *stand clear*

the panicked slam of my desperate hands / haul her back from the tunnel /
    the rib snapped shut / a sudden myocardiogram paddles back to life

and Small is back, laughing her head off

NOTES

Bodkin
A **bodkin** is a thick, blunt needle, often used to test if a woman was a witch in the Middle Ages. If no blood was drawn, she was accused.

There Are No Daffodils in Varanasi
Gulab jamun is a deep-fried, milk-based doughnut popular in India.
Banaras is another name for the city of Varanasi.
Assi Ghat refers to the southernmost ghat in Varanasi.

Fugu
Fugu is a pufferfish, which is served as a Japanese delicacy. It's reported to be more poisonous than cyanide if not prepared correctly.

Better Lies
Lassi is a yoghurt-based drink from India, often made with water, spices and fruit.
Jhal muri is a street food snack from Bengal usually consisting of a mix of puffed rice, vegetables, spices and nuts.

Hemkomst
Hemkomst is a Swedish word, meaning 'homecoming'.
Min vän is the Swedish for 'my friend'.
Hem is Swedish for 'him'.

ACKNOWLEDGEMENTS

Acknowledgement is due to the publications in which some of these poems first appeared. These include *New Welsh Review*, *Poetry Wales*, *The Lonely Crowd*, *Inside the Bell Jar*, *Black Bough* and *Southword Journal*. 'Adders' was shortlisted for the Yeovil Prize 2019. 'Andromache' was shortlisted for the York Literature Festival Prize 2018. 'Achilles' made the finals of the Cursed Murphy Spoken Word Award 2020 and 'Better Lies' was shortlisted for the Anthony Cronin International Poetry Prize.

Huge thanks is due to my wonderful editor Susie Wildsmith for her sharp observational eye, constant encouragement and unwavering support. This book wouldn't have been the same without all your help over the years. Thank you also to the brilliant Richard Davies and Team Parthian for their tireless hard work, for always believing in me as a writer and for becoming friends as well as publishers.

Thanks are due to my beautiful family: Mam, Dad, Nan, Woofy, Em, Chris and Callum. Thanks also to my brilliant friends and, I suppose, to the cat (you're not having another treat though, you're already the size of a small bear).

Thank you to my Salty Poets: Rhys Owain Williams, Mari Ellis Dunning, Emily Vanderploeg, Adam Sillman, Alan Kellermann and Rae Howells for your honesty, support and … well, sass. I am ever grateful to Aida Birch and the *Cheval* judges and trustees, and am honoured to be a part of your wonderful work today. To Bee Books, British Council, VCV Wales and Literature Wales, for making me fall in love with India. To Sophie McKeand, Siôn Tomos Owen, Gary Raymond, Rebecca Gould, Esha Chatterjee, Sugandha Bandyopadhyay and Aniesha Brahma for making it even better.

Always grateful to Luke Clement, Rhea Seren Phillips, Lee Prosser, Oliver James Lomax, Jonathan Edwards, Hazel Duke, Jonathan Richards, Shehzar Doja, Molly Holborn, Dominic Williams, Donald H Taylor and John Goodby for your constant encouragement. Every single kind word and piece of advice has truly made a difference. To my beloved Swansea (and Swedish) poetry community – keep lifting each other like you've done for so many years for me.

To Liz, Helen and Beat Support, for going above and beyond during the worst times with Small.

To Ian Llewellyn, for your patience, selflessness, humour and support (even if you don't like 'the ones without rhymes').

Thank you to Roisin O'Connor and Zoe Alford, the two talented and brilliant women who bring out the best in me.

And finally, to Anthony Jones, Mark Montinaro and Nigel Jenkins. Never, ever forgotten.

PARTHIAN *Poetry in Translation*

Home on the Move
Two poems go on a journey
Edited by Manuela Perteghella
and Ricarda Vidal
ISBN 978-1-912681-46-4
£8.99 | Paperback
'One of the most inventive and necessary
poetry projects of recent years...'
– Chris McCabe

Pomegranate Garden
A selection of poems by Haydar Ergülen
Edited by Mel Kenne, Saliha Paker
and Caroline Stockford
ISBN 978-1-912681-42-6
£8.99 | Paperback
'A major poet who rises from [his] roots to touch
on what is human at its most stripped-down,
vulnerable and universal...'
– Michel Cassir, *L'Harmattan*

Modern Bengali Poetry
Arunava Sinha
ISBN 978-1-912681-22-8
£11.99 | Paperback
This volume celebrates over one hundred years
of poetry from the two Bengals represented
by over fifty different poets.

PARTHIAN *Poetry*

Hey Bert
Roberto Pastore
ISBN 978-1-912109-34-0
£9.00 | Paperback
'Bert's writing, quite simply, makes me happy.
Jealous but happy.'
– Crystal Jeans

Sliced Tongue and Pearl Cufflinks
Kittie Belltree
ISBN 978-1-912681-14-3
£9.00 | Paperback
'By turns witty and sophisticated, her writing shivers
with a suggestion of unease that is compelling.'
– Samantha Wynne-Rhydderch

Hymns Ancient & Modern
New & Selected Poems
J. Brookes
ISBN 978-1-912681-33-4
£9.99 | Paperback
'It's a skilful writer indeed who can combine elements both
heartbreaking and hilarious: Brookes is that writer.'
– Robert Minhinnick

How to Carry Fire
Christina Thatcher
ISBN 978-1-912681-48-8
£9.00 | Paperback
'A dazzling array of poems both remarkable in their ingenuity,
and raw, unforgettable honesty.'
– Helen Calcutt